Poems about Feelings
Mud Between the Toes

Chosen by Wendy Cooling

Illustrated by Anthony Lewis

FRANKLIN WATTS
NEW YORK • LONDON • SYDNEY

First published in 2000 by Franklin Watts
96, Leonard Street, London EC2A 4XD

Franklin Watts Australia
14 Mars Road, Lane Cove, NSW 2066

© in this anthology Wendy Cooling 2000
Illustration © Anthony Lewis 2000

Editor: Sarah Snashall
Designer: Louise Thomas
Border artwork: Diana Mayo

ISBN 0 7496 3479 0

Dewey classification 821.008

Printed in Hong Kong/China

Acknowledgments

The editor and publishers gratefully acknowledge
permission to reproduce the following copyright material.

Summer, by Frank Asch, from *Country Pie*, 1979.
Reprinted with permission of Greenwillow Books, a
division of William Morrow & Co. *No Haiku*, by Adrian
Henri. Permission granted by the author. *Garden Hose*,
by Ifor Thomas. Permission granted by the author. *I'm
Just Going Out*, by Michael Rosen, from *Wouldn't You
Like to Know?* Permission granted by Scholastic Ltd.
A Great Discovery, by Paul Rogers. First published in
Yuck, by Thomas Nelson, 1993. Permission granted by
the author. *Some Things Don't Make Any Sense At All*,
by Judith Viorst from *If I Were In Charge of the World
and other Worries*. Published by Atheneum Books for
Young Readers, an imprint of Simon & Schuster
Children's Publishing Division. © 1981 Judith Viorst.
This usage granted by permission. *Lemons*, by Patricia
Hubbell, from *The Apple Vendor's Fair*, by Patricia
Hubbell. © 1963, 1991 Patricia Hubbell. Used by
permission of Marian Reiner for the author. *Happy
Birthday, Dilroy!* by John Agard, from *I Din Do Nuttin*,
The Bodley Head. Permission granted by The Bodley
Head. *Chicken Spots*, by Peter Dixon. Permission
granted by the author. *Shoes*, by John Foster. Permission
granted by the author. *What Are Little Girls...*, by Adrian
Henri. Permission granted by the author. *In This Tree*, by
June Crebbin, from *Cows Moo, Cars Toot*, by June
Crebbin (Viking, 1995). © June Crebbin, 1995. *Rolling
Down a Hill*, by Colin West. Permission granted by the
author. *Shallow Poem*, by Gerda Mayer. Permission
granted by the author. *Monday Morning*, by John C.
Head. Reprinted with permission of John C. Head.
Storytime, by Judith Nicholls. © 1987. From *Midnight
Forest*, by Judith Nicholls, published by Faber & Faber.
Reprinted by permission of the author. *Out of School*, by
Hal Summers. Permission granted by the author.

Every effort has been made to trace copyright, but if any
omissions have been made please let us know in order
that we may put it right in the next edition.

Contents

Boys and Girls Come Out to Play

Boys and girls come out to play,
The moon doth shine as bright as day.
Leave your supper, and leave your sleep,
And join your playfellows in the street.
Come with a whoop, and come with a call,
Come with a good will or not at all.
Up the ladder and down the wall,
A half-penny loaf will serve us all.
You find milk, and I'll find flour,
And we'll have a pudding in half an hour.

Traditional

Wakey, Wakey

Wakey, wakey, rise and shine,
Make your bed,
And then make mine.

Anon

Mud

I like mud.
  I like it on my clothes.
I like it on my fingers.
  I like it in my toes.

Dirt's pretty ordinary
  And dust's a dud.
For a really good mess-up
  I like mud.

by John Smith

Summer

When it's hot
I take my shoes off,
I take my shirt off,
I take my pants off,
I take my underwear off,
I take my whole body off,
and throw it
in the river.

by Frank Asch

No Haiku

I'm sorry to say
that I really don't feel like
a haiku today.

by Adrian Henri

Where Go the Boats?

Dark brown is the river,
    Golden is the sand.
It flows along for ever,
    With trees on either hand.

Green leaves a-floating,
    Castles of the foam,
Boats of mine a-boating –
    Where will all come home?

On goes the river
    And out past the mill,
Away down the valley,
    Away down the hill.

Away down the river,
    A hundred miles or more,
Other little children
    Shall bring my boats ashore.

by Robert Louis Stevenson

Garden Hose

There's something sneaky about a garden hose
coiled on the lawn next to the climbing rose
the colour of something out of your nose,
like a lazy snake having a doze.
But when the tap's turned on and the water flows
it'll jump out of your hands and wet your toes.
Be careful to check which way the wind blows
or you'll be back inside to change your clothes.
And then you'll know what everyone knows,
there's something sneaky about a garden hose.

by Ifor Thomas

I'm Just Going Out

I'm just going out for a moment.
Why?
To make a cup of tea.
Why?
Because I'm thirsty.
Why?
Because it's hot.
    Why?

        Because the sun's shining.
          Why?
            Because it's summer.
          Why?
           Because that's when it is.
        Why?
Why don't you stop saying why?
Why?
Tea-time why.
High-time-you-stopped-saying-why-time.
What?

by Michael Rosen

A Great Discovery

I've made a great discovery,
proved beyond all doubt.
What I did to prove it
nearly wore me out.

Sides and armpits, knees
                    and feet
– I tried it everywhere.
Standing, sitting, lying down;
I tried it dressed *and* bare.

I tried it every way I could.
That's how I know it's true.
And just to check, I went and asked
my friends to try it too.

It can't be done – it really can't.
All of them agree.
I'm ready now to tell the world
my great discovery:
You cannot tickle yourself.

by Paul Rogers

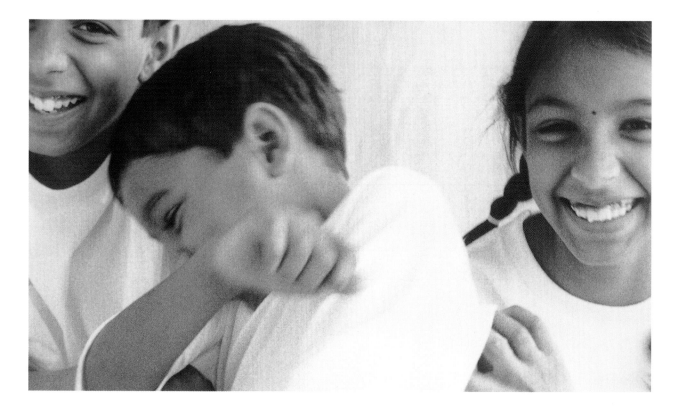

Tumbling

In jumping and tumbling
  We spend the whole day,
Till night by arriving
  Has finished our play.

What then? One and all,
  There's no more to be said,
As we tumbled all day,
  So we tumble to bed.

Anon

Mashed Potato - Love Poem

If I ever had to choose between you
and a third helping of mashed potato,
(whipped lightly with a fork
not whisked,
and a little pool of butter
melting in the middle...)

I think
I'd choose
the mashed potato.

But I'd choose you next.

by Sidney Hodder

Some Things Don't Make
Any Sense At All

My mom says I'm her sugarplum.

My mom says I'm her lamb.

My mom says I'm completely perfect

Just the way I am.

My mom says I'm a super-special wonderful terrific little guy.

My mom just had another baby.

Why?

by Judith Viorst

Lemons

A lemon's a lemony kind of a thing,
It doesn't look sharp and it doesn't look sting,
It looks rather round and it looks rather square,
It looks almost oval, a yellowy pear.
It looks like a waxy old, yellow old pear,
It looks like a pear without any stem,
It doesn't look sharp and it doesn't look sting,
A lemon's a lemony kind of a thing.
But cut it and taste it and touch it with tongue
You'll see where the sharp and the sting have
   been hiding –
Under the yellow without any warning;
I touch it and touch it again with my tongue,
I like it! I like it! I like to be stung!

by Patricia Hubbell

14

Peas

I eat my peas with honey,
I've done it all my life;
It makes my peas taste funny,
But it keeps them on the knife.

Anon

Mary Had a Little Lamb

Mary had a little lamb,
   A lobster and some prunes,
A glass of milk, a piece of pie,
   And then some macaroons.

It made the busy waiters grin
   To see her order so,
And when they carried Mary out,
   Her face was white as snow.

Anon

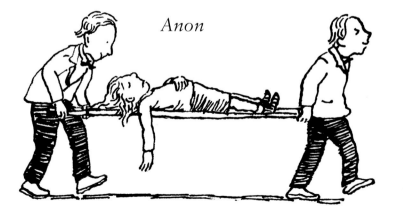

Betty at the Party

"When I was at the party,"
　　　Said Betty, aged just four,
"A little girl fell off her chair
　　　Right down upon the floor;
And all the other little girls
　　　Began to laugh, but me –
I didn't laugh a single bit,"
　　　Said Betty seriously.

"Why not?" her mother asked her,
　　　Full of delight to find
That Betty – bless her little heart! –
　　　Had been so sweetly kind.
"Why didn't you laugh, my darling?
　　　Or don't you like to tell?"
"I didn't laugh," said Betty,
　　　"'Cause me it was that fell."

Anon

Happy Birthday, Dilroy!

My name is Dilroy.
I'm a little black boy
and I'm eight today.

My birthday cards say
it's great to be eight
and they sure right
coz I got a pair of skates
I want for a long time.

My birthday cards say,
Happy Birthday, Dilroy!
But, Mummy, tell me why
they don't put a little boy
that looks a bit like me.
Why the boy on the card so white?

by John Agard

Chicken Spots

I've got these really itchy spots
they're climbing on my tummy
they're on my head
they're on my tail
and it isn't very funny.
They came to see me yesterday
– a few the day before
fifty on my bottom
and twenty on my jaw.

I've got a prize one on my toe
a dozen on my knee
and now they're on my thingy
– I think there's thirty-three.

I count them every evening
I give them names like Fred
Charlie Di and Daisy
Chunky Tom and Ted.

They're really awful spotties
they drive me itchy mad
the sort of itchy scratchings
I wish I never had.
Nobby's worst at itching
Lizzie's awful too
and – if you come to see me
Then I'll give a few to you...

I'll give you Di and Daisy –
I'll give you Jane and Ted
a bucket full of itchers
to take home to your bed...
    You can give them to your sister
      I don't care what you do
      give them to a teacher
      or send them to the zoo.
      I don't care where you take 'em
      I don't care where they go...
        stick them up the chimney
        or in the baby's po.
        Take them to a farmyard.
        Find a chicken pen,
        say that they're a present

        with love
        from me

          ...to them.

by Peter Dixon

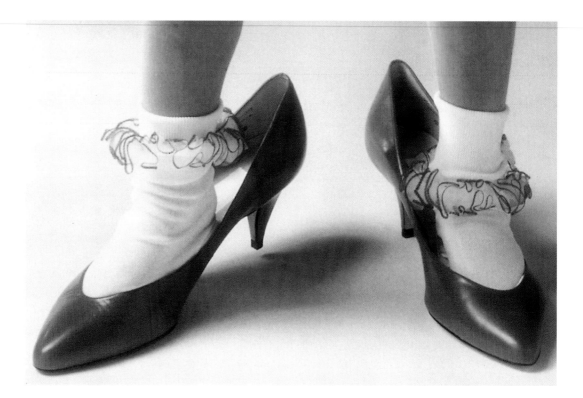

Shoes

Red shoes, blue shoes,
Old shoes, new shoes.

Shoes that are comfy,
Shoes that are tight,
Shoes that are black,
Shoes that are white.

Shoes with buckles,
Shoes with bows,
Shoes that are narrow
And pinch your toes.

Shoes that are yellow,
Shoes that are green,
Shoes that are dirty,
Shoes that are clean.

Shoes for when it's cold,
Shoes for when it's hot.
Shoes with laces
That get tangled in a knot!

by John Foster

My New Shoes

My shoes are new and squeaky shoes,
They're very shiny, creaky shoes,
I wish I had my leaky shoes
That Mummy threw away.

I liked my old brown leaky shoes
Much better than these creaky shoes,
These shiny, creaky, squeaky shoes
I've got to wear today.

Anon

creak: squeak

What Are Little Girls...

I'm not
a
sugar and spice
girl
an all-things nice
girl
a do-as-told
good-as-gold
pretty frock
never shock
girl

I'm
a
slugs and snails
girl
a puppy-dog's-tails
girl
a climbing trees
dirty knees
hole-in-sock
love-to-shock
girl

cricket bats
and big white rats
crested newts
and football boots

that's what
this little girl's

...MADE OF.

by Adrian Henri

Tommy

Young Tommy would not go to bed,
But sat watching TV instead,
    As he stayed up to stare
    His face went all square
And aerials grew from his head.

Anon

In This Tree

In this tree
are greenflies, sawflies
and beetles burrowing,

In this tree
are ferns and mosses
and a thread of honeysuckle,

In this tree
are butterflies
feeding on sunlit leaves,

woodpeckers
searching for insects,

squirrels nesting,

In this tree
are acorns
and a notice saying:
BULL IN FIELD.

What's that noise?
What's that thundering noise
behind me?

Help!

In this tree
are all these things

and me.

by June Crebbin

Rolling Down a Hill

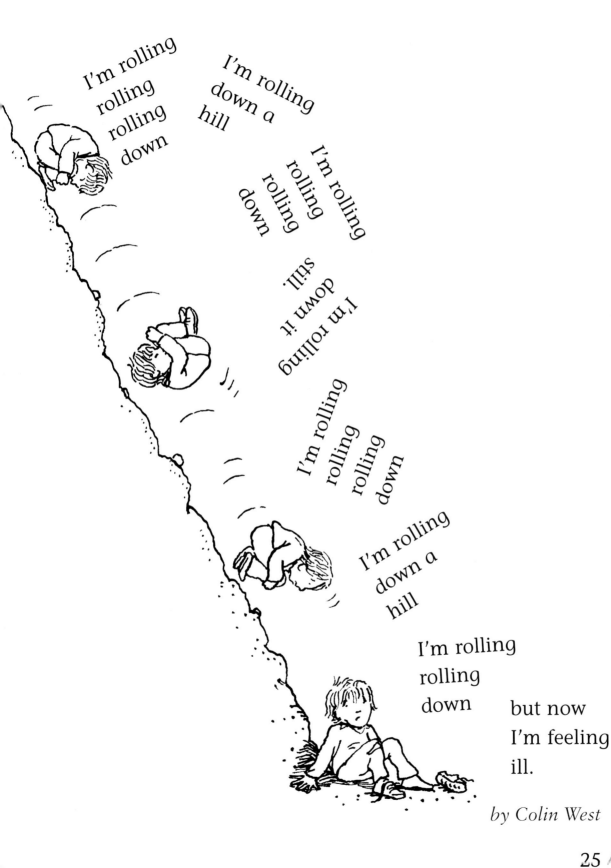

I'm rolling
rolling
rolling
down

I'm rolling
down a
hill

I'm rolling
rolling
rolling
down

I'm rolling
down it
still.

I'm rolling
rolling
rolling
down

I'm rolling
down a
hill

I'm rolling
rolling
down

but now
I'm feeling
ill.

by Colin West

Shallow Poem

I've thought of a poem.
I carry it carefully,
nervously, in my head,
like a saucer of milk;
in case I should spill some lines
before I can put it down.

by Gerda Mayer

Monday Morning

Moaning, groaning,
mumbling, grumbling,
glowering, showering,
rubbing, scrubbing,
washing, sploshing,
groping, soaping,
howling, towelling,
splashing, dashing,
muttering, buttering,
crunching, munching,
sighing, tying,
brushing, rushing,
cramming, slamming
and off to
school.

by John C. Head

Storytime

Once upon a time, children,
there lived a fearsome dragon...

Please, miss,
Jamie's made a dragon.
Out in the sandpit.

Lovely, Andrew.
Now this dragon
had enormous red eyes
and a swirling, whirling tail...

Jamie's dragon's got
yellow eyes, miss.

Lovely, Andrew.
Now this dragon was
as wide as a horse
as green as the grass
as tall as a house...

Jamie's would JUST fit
in our classroom, miss!

But he was a very friendly dragon...

Jamie's dragon ISN'T, miss.
He eats people, miss.
Especially TEACHERS,
Jamie said.

Very nice, Andrew!

Now one day, children,
this enormous dragon
rolled his red eye,
whirled his swirly green tail
and set off to find...

His dinner, miss!
Because he was hungry, miss!

Thank you, Andrew.
He rolled his red eye,
whirled his green tail,
and opened his wide, wide mouth
until

oooooooaaah

Please, miss,
I did try to tell you, miss!

by Judith Nicholls

What Teachers Dream

Teachers dream of 4 o'clock
and coffee lightly stirred,
they dream of quiet children
who hardly say a word.

They dream of summer holidays
and chairs which never scrape,
they dream of no wet playtimes
and children never late.

They dream of banning bubble gum
they dream of playing pool
but, mostly, teachers dream
of there being no more school.

by Andrew Collett

Out of School

Four o'clock strikes
There's a rising hum,
Then the doors fly open
The children come.

With a wild cat-call
And a hop-scotch hop
And a bouncing ball
And a whirling top.

Grazing of knees
A hair-pull and a slap,
A hitched up satchel,
A pulled down cap,

Bully boys reeling off
Hurt ones squealing off,
Aviators wheeling off,
Mousy ones stealing off,

Woollen gloves for chilblains,
Cotton rags for snufflers,
Pig-tails, coat-tails,
Tails of mufflers.

Machine gun cries
A kennelful of snarlings
A hurricane of leaves
A tree of starlings,

Thinning away now
By some and some,
Thinning away, away,
All gone home.

by Hal Summers

Index of First Lines

Picture credits

Cover image and title page:
Robert Harding (Julia Bayne)

Inside images:
Bubbles p.5 (Ian West)
Eye Ubiquitous p.14 (Paul Seheult)
Franklin Watts p.30 (Harry Cory-Wright)
Image Bank pp. 6, 11 (Steve Satushek),
20 (Howard Berman)
Rex Interstock p.8 (Vic Thomassen)
Robert Harding pp. 10, 24, 31
(Bildagentur Schuster/Dr. Müller)
Tony Stone pp. 17 (Lori Adamski Peek),
22 (Herman Agopian), 27 (Nancy Honey)